D1071176

DEMCO

★ ★ ★ ★ ★ ★ ★ ★ ★ ★ ★ ★ ★ ★ ★ ★ ★ ★ ★ ★ ★ ★ ★ ★ ★ ★ ★ ★ ★

# TENNESSEE

by Patricia Lantier

GARETH**STEVENS**
PUBLISHING
A Member of the WRC Media Family of Companies

Please visit our web site at: www.garethstevens.com
For a free color catalog describing Gareth Stevens Publishing's
list of high-quality books and multimedia programs, call
1-800-542-2595 (USA) or 1-800-387-3178 (Canada).
Gareth Stevens Publishing's fax: (414) 332-3567.

Library of Congress Cataloging-in-Publication Data

Lantier, Patricia, 1952-
    Tennessee / Patricia Lantier.
      p. cm. — (Portraits of the states)
    Includes bibliographical references and index.
    ISBN 0-8368-4634-6 (lib. bdg.)
    ISBN 0-8368-4653-2 (softcover)
    1. Tennessee—Juvenile literature. I. Title. II. Series.
    F436.3.L34   2005
    976.8—dc22                 2005045157

This edition first published in 2006 by
**Gareth Stevens Publishing**
A Member of the WRC Media Family of Companies
330 West Olive Street, Suite 100
Milwaukee, WI 53212 USA

This edition copyright © 2006 by Gareth Stevens, Inc.

Editorial direction: Mark J. Sachner
Project manager: Jonatha A. Brown
Editor: Betsy Rasmussen
Art direction and design: Tammy West
Picture research: Diane Laska-Swanke
Indexer: Walter Kronenberg
Production: Jessica Morris and Robert Kraus

Picture credits: Cover, © Frank Micelotta/Getty Images; p. 4 © James P. Rowan;
p. 5 © Corel; p. 6 © Hulton Archive/Getty Images; p. 9 © Art Today; p. 11
© MPI/Getty Images; p. 12 © Frank Driggs Collection/Getty Images; pp. 15, 19,
21, 22, 24, 26 © Gibson Stock Photography; p. 16 © Library of Congress; pp. 17,
25 © North Wind Picture Archives; p. 27 © Neil Brake/AFP/Getty Images; p. 28
© PhotoDisc; p. 29 © IOC/Getty Images

Printed in the United States of America

1 2 3 4 5 6 7 8 9 09 08 07 06 05

# CONTENTS

Words that are defined in the Glossary appear
in **bold** the first time they are used in the text.

On the Cover: The Grand Ole Opry House in Nashville hosts many
country western music concerts and awards ceremonies.

# Introduction

**I**f you could visit Tennessee, where would you go? The Smoky Mountains? Graceland? The Lost Sea? The Grand Ole Opry? Tennessee has many fun places to visit.

Tennessee is a state with great natural beauty. It has mountains, valleys, fertile **soil**, and a mild climate. It also has a rich culture of music, sports, and crafts.

The people of Tennessee are strong and **independent**. Early settlers in the state farmed on land new to them. They worked hard to survive on their own. But these **pioneers** also had the spirit of adventure.

The pioneers were always ready to help others, too. The same is true of the people living there today. Welcome to Tennessee, the Volunteer State!

The Great Smoky Mountains National Park is protected by the U.S. government. It is a paradise for people who love nature. The park has over 800 miles (1,290 kilometers) of hiking trails.

The state flag of Tennessee.

# TENNESSEE FACTS

- Became the 16th U.S. state: June 1, 1796
- Population (2004): 5,900,962
- Capital: Nashville
- Biggest Cities: Memphis, Nashville, Knoxville, Chattanooga
- Size: 41,217 square miles (106,752 square kilometers)
- Nickname: The Volunteer State
- State Tree: Tulip poplar
- State Flower: Iris
- State Animal: Raccoon
- State Bird: Mockingbird

# History

**N**ative Americans first came to Tennessee thousands of years ago. The earliest Native group lived by hunting. Later, a group of Natives called Mound Builders lived there. They began farming. They grew squash, corn, and beans. These Natives also built large **mounds**. The mounds were important to their religion. Other Native American groups later lived in the area. The most powerful was the Cherokee.

John Sevier was a soldier and political leader. He helped Tennessee become a state.

## Explorers and Settlers

Spanish explorers came to Tennessee in 1540. Hernando de Soto led the group. These men were looking for gold and silver, they brought diseases with them. Many Natives died from these diseases. The explorers also brought guns with them. Guns changed the ways the Natives hunted for food and fought wars.

People from other countries came later. In 1682, French explorer Robert de La

Salle claimed the land now known as Tennessee for France. Soon, French settlers began to move to the area.

The French traded with the Natives for furs. The British also wanted furs. Some Natives traded with the French, and others traded with the British. The French and British both wanted to own the land. A war between France and Britain began in 1754. It was called the French and Indian War. Many Natives fought on the side of the French. Great Britain won the war. It now held most of the land in eastern North America. This land included the Tennessee region.

In the 1760s, settlers from the British **colonies** on the East Coast began moving into the Tennessee area. Some of these settlers brought African American slaves with them to work on

### IN TENNESSEE'S HISTORY

**Freedom Fighter**
Davy Crockett was born in Limestown in 1786. He was a famous **scout** and hunter. He liked to tell stories about his adventures. Crockett served in the U.S. House of Representatives. He also tried to help Native Americans. Some people did not like this. Crockett helped the people of Texas fight for freedom. In 1836, he died at the Battle of the Alamo in Texas.

## IN TENNESSEE'S HISTORY

**Pathfinder**

Daniel Boone was a famous scout. He explored wild areas of North America. He also made paths for settlers to follow. When people wanted to move to Tennessee and farther West, they did not know how to cross the Appalachian Mountains. Daniel Boone was hired to make a trail over the mountains for new settlers to follow. It was named the Wilderness Trail. People were able to cross the mountains through a pass called the Cumberland Gap. This brought them into Tennessee.

large farms. As more and more people moved to the area, they needed more and more land. The Natives finally sold some of their land.

People living in the British colonies fought against Britain in the Revolutionary War. The colonies wanted to be independent from Britain. Some people from Tennessee helped fight this war. The Americans won the war in 1783. The colonies became the United States of America.

## Territory and Statehood

The U.S. government named the Tennessee area the **Territory** South of the River Ohio in 1790. Thousands of people moved to this new territory. Tennessee became the sixteenth state on June 1, 1796. John Sevier was the state's first governor.

## Time of Loss

The United States went to war with Great Britain again in the War of 1812. Andrew Jackson from Tennessee became a hero in this war. He would later become president of the United States.

When the war ended, more settlers came to the state. The U.S. government passed the Indian Removal Act in 1830. Natives in Tennessee had to move farther west. The Cherokee signed a **treaty** giving up their land. They were forced to walk about 1,000 miles (1,609 kilometers) to a new home. Many of them died along the way. The march became known as the Trail of Tears.

### Divided Land

Northern states did not allow slavery. Southern states wanted to keep slavery. The South broke away and formed their own country, called the Confederate States of America. Northern states did not want the country to split. Civil war began in the United States in 1861.

Tennessee fought for the South in the Civil War. The war lasted four years. More than two hundred battles were fought in Tennessee.

### Brave Soldiers

The state's governor asked people to fight in the War of 1812. So many men signed up to fight that Tennessee was named the Volunteer State.

Major General Andrew Jackson became a hero in the War of 1812. He led his forces to defeat the British at the Battle of New Orleans.

## Famous People of Tennessee

### Andrew Jackson

**Born:** March 15, 1767, Waxhaw, South Carolina

**Died:** June 8, 1845, the Hermitage (near Nashville), Tennessee

Andrew Jackson moved to Tennessee when he was twenty-one years old. He worked as a lawyer. He fought in the War of 1812 and became a hero. After the war, Jackson was a leader in the state. In 1828, he was elected president of the United States. He served two terms.

industries. Railroads were built and made it possible to move people and goods from one area of the country to another.

## A New Century

World War I and World War II were fought in the first half of the twentieth century. These wars took place in Europe and other countries. U.S. soldiers from Tennessee fought in both of these wars.

The North won, and slavery ended. Tennessee was the first Southern state to rejoin the Union.

The state continued to grow after the Civil War. Settlers farmed or mined for coal. They also worked in the iron and steel

### IN TENNESSEE'S HISTORY

**Power Play**

U.S. president Abraham Lincoln was killed a few days after the Civil War ended. Vice President Andrew Johnson from Tennessee became president. President Johnson had a plan to rebuild the country, but some people did not like the plan. They tried to push Johnson out of office. They did not succeed. He remained president.

The Battle of Shiloh was fought in 1862 near the Tennessee River. More than ten thousand men from both the North and the South were injured or killed in the fighting. Neither side won the battle.

The **Great Depression** began in the United States in the early 1930s. During this time, the prices paid for goods fell. People lost their jobs. President Franklin D. Roosevelt had a plan. It was called the New Deal. Part of the New Deal was the Tennessee Valley Authority (TVA). As part of the TVA, the government helped the people of Tennessee.

Workers were hired to build **dams** along the Tennessee River. This created jobs. The dams used moving water to create electricity, so more people had electricity in their homes. The dams also helped control flooding. This protected crops and homes from being destroyed by rising water.

## Equal Rights

Even though slavery had ended, African Americans still did not have many rights. In the 1950s, they began to push for equality. The laws slowly changed. A sad event happened in 1968. Dr. Martin Luther King Jr., a famous black leader, was

## Famous People of Tennessee

### Elvis Aaron Presley

**Born:** January 8, 1935, Tupelo, Mississippi

**Died:** August 16, 1977, Memphis, Tennessee

Elvis Presley is called "the King of Rock and Roll." He listened to gospel and blues music in Memphis as he grew up. Then, he began singing his own type of music. Young people all over the country loved his songs. Elvis sold more than one billion records. Two of his most popular songs were "Heartbreak Hotel" and "Blue Suede Shoes." He also became a movie star. Fans now can visit his home, named Graceland.

shot and killed in Memphis. African Americans today have the same rights as all other people in the country.

### Today in Tennessee

Tennessee still has farms, but it also has **factories** and big businesses. Factories make many products, such as clothing, auto parts, tents, and boats. The Nissan automobile company is making one of its plants larger. It will open in 2006.

Elvis Presley sang and acted in the movie *Jailhouse Rock*.

# ★ ★ ★ Time Line ★ ★ ★

| | |
|---|---|
| **1540** | Hernando de Soto leads a group of Spanish explorers through the Tennessee area. |
| **1682** | French explorer Robert de La Salle claims the land of Tennessee for France. |
| **1796** | Tennessee becomes the sixteenth state. |
| **1812–1814** | The War of 1812 takes place between the United States and Britain. Andrew Jackson from Tennessee becomes a hero in this war. |
| **1830** | The U.S. government passes the Indian Removal Act. Natives from Tennessee are forced to march on what has become known as the Trail of Tears. |
| **1861–1865** | The Civil War is fought with more than two hundred battles occurring in Tennessee. |
| **1933** | President Franklin D. Roosevelt establishes the Tennessee Valley Authority, providing jobs for Tennessee workers. |
| **1968** | Dr. Martin Luther King Jr. is shot and killed in Memphis. |
| **1992** | Albert Gore Jr. of Tennessee is elected vice president of the United States under President Bill Clinton. |
| **1997** | The Ohio River overflows its banks, flooding many cities in Tennessee. |

# People

Nearly six million people live in Tennessee. Native Americans were the first to live there. Later, settlers moved to the area from the British colonies and Europe. The Natives sold some of their land to the settlers, but the settlers demanded more and more land. Most of the Natives were forced to move away. Today, only a small part of the state's **population** is Native American.

**Hispanics:** In the 2000 U.S. Census, 2.2 percent of the people living in Tennessee called themselves Latino or Hispanic. Most of them or their relatives came from places where Spanish is spoken. They may come from different racial backgrounds.

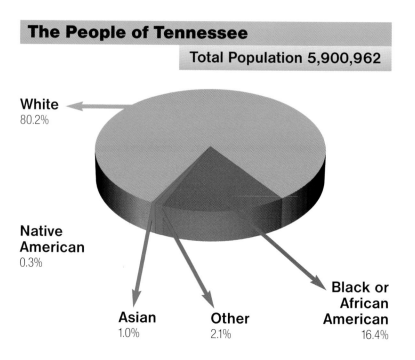

## The People of Tennessee

**Total Population 5,900,962**

White 80.2%

Native American 0.3%

Asian 1.0%

Other 2.1%

Black or African American 16.4%

Percentages are based on 2000 Census.

Memphis is a busy port on the Mississippi River. It has a strong economy and many exciting attractions for visitors and the people who live there.

Most of the state's early settlers were Europeans. Some came from England and Ireland. Others came from France and Germany. Many of these people lived in the colonies before moving west to Tennessee. Later, people moved to the state from other areas of the world.

About 80 percent of the people in Tennessee are white. More than 16 percent are African American. Smaller numbers of people in the state belong to other races.

The early settlers were farmers. Most of the settlers who moved there lived in **rural** areas. Farming is still a part of life for many people, but today more than half of the people in the state live in or near cities.

Memphis and Nashville are the state's largest cities. Memphis is in the south-

**Many people in Tennessee enjoy getting together and "making music." This is especially true in the rural areas of the state.**

western part of the state. Nashville is in the middle part of the state. More than one million people live in each of these cities and their surrounding areas. The region around Nashville, called the Nashville Basin, is the fastest-growing part of the state.

## Education

A free education was offered to all children in Tennessee in 1873. Taxes paid for the schools. The state was one of the first in the South to say every child must go to school. This became a law in 1913. The state has a program called "Better Schools." Its purpose is to improve education in the state. It is a good model for other schools in the country. Tax money is used to help make the program work.

The state has strong colleges and universities.

## Famous People of Tennessee

### Sequoyah

**Born:** About 1770, Taskigi, North Carolina colony

**Died:** August 1843, near San Fernando, Mexico

Sequoyah was born in a small village. His father was a white trader. His mother was the daughter of a Cherokee chief. Sequoyah never went to school. He worked as a silversmith and trader. He also had the name George Gist. Sequoyah became interested in the English written language. He then developed a Cherokee alphabet. First, he taught the alphabet to his daughter. Then, he taught thousands of Cherokee to read and write.

Vanderbilt University and the University of Tennessee are well known. Fisk University is one of the oldest African American colleges in the country.

## Religion

About 90 percent of the people in Tennessee are Christians. Nearly 67 percent of these Christians are Baptists or Southern Baptists. More than 10 percent are Methodists, and about 5 percent are Catholics. Smaller numbers are Jews, Muslims, and Buddhists.

Sequoyah spent twelve years working on the Cherokee writing system.

# The Land

Tennessee has three main regions. They are called East, Middle, and West Tennessee. Huge pieces of ice called **glaciers** helped form these areas, but each area has a different look.

East Tennessee has mountains and forests. The Great Smoky Mountains form the eastern **border** of the state. The highest point is Clingmans Dome. It rises 6,643 feet (2,025 meters) above sea level.

Middle Tennessee has deep valleys. The Cumberland River flows through this area. The Tennessee River forms a western edge for this region. The soil there is good for farming. The Cumberland **Plateau** is an area of valleys that sits between flat-topped mountains. The state capital, Nashville, is in Middle Tennessee.

West Tennessee has low, flat land. The Mississippi River forms the western border of the state. This area has rich soil for farming. Memphis, the largest city in the state, is in West Tennessee.

## FUN FACTS

### Hidden Lake

The Lost Sea is the largest underground lake in the United States. It is in Sweetwater, a city in the eastern part of the state. A saber-toothed tiger was an early visitor to the Lost Sea. Its bones are in a museum. Visitors can walk through underground rooms around the lake. They also can ride on the lake in glass-bottom boats.

# TENNESSEE

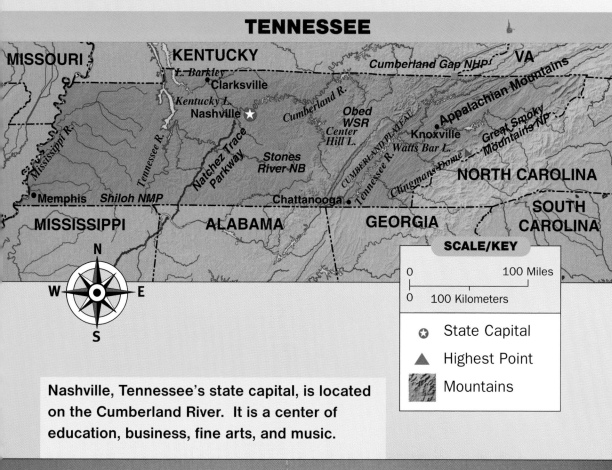

MISSOURI

KENTUCKY

VA

Cumberland Gap NHP

L. Barkley

Clarksville

Kentucky L.

Cumberland R.

Nashville ⭐

Cumberland R.

Appalachian Mountains

Obed WSR

Knoxville

Great Smoky Mountains NP

Mississippi R.

Tennessee R.

Center Hill L.

Watts Bar L.

Natchez Trace Parkway

Stones River NB

CUMBERLAND PLATEAU

Tennessee R.

Clingmans Dome ▲

NORTH CAROLINA

Memphis

Shiloh NMP

Chattanooga

SOUTH CAROLINA

MISSISSIPPI

ALABAMA

GEORGIA

**N**
**W** ✸ **E**
**S**

### SCALE/KEY

0 ⟷ 100 Miles

0 ⟷ 100 Kilometers

⭐ State Capital

▲ Highest Point

🏔 Mountains

Nashville, Tennessee's state capital, is located on the Cumberland River. It is a center of education, business, fine arts, and music.

## Climate

The state has a mild climate. Summers are warm, and winters are cool. Areas in the mountains have the coldest weather. The state receives about 45 inches (114 centimeters) of rain

| Major Rivers |
| --- |
| **Mississippi River** 2,357 miles (3,792 km) long |
| **Cumberland River** 687 miles (1,105 km) long |
| **Tennessee River** 652 miles (1,049 km) long |

a year. Some snow falls each year in most parts of the state. The mountains always receive the most snow.

## Waterways

Tennessee has thousands of miles of rivers and streams. The three major rivers in the state help move goods from one place to another. The Mississippi River is the longest river. It forms the state's western border. Parts of the Tennessee River flow through the eastern and western areas of the state. The Cumberland River flows east to west.

**FUN FACTS**

### Earthquake!

Some of the worst earthquakes in U.S. history happened in the winter of 1811–1812. They were near the northwest corner of Tennessee. The quakes caused a huge wave on the Mississippi River. The water then moved backward. It filled up an area of land that had dropped several feet. This created Reelfoot Lake. Reelfoot Lake is special for another reason. Large numbers of bald eagles visit the lake every winter.

The Tennessee Walking Horse is a mix of early horses that came to the region. This type of horse is known mainly for its fast running walk. It can walk up to 12 miles (19 km) an hour.

The state also has many beautiful lakes. The largest natural lake is Reelfoot Lake.

## Plants and Animals

Forests cover about one-half of the state. More than two hundred kinds of trees grow there. Plants such as azaleas, rhododendrons, and mountain laurels also grow in the state. Daisies, poppies, and coneflowers are just some of the wildflowers that grow in the state.

Many kinds of birds live in Tennessee. Wild ducks, pheasant, geese, and quail live in several areas. Other songbirds living there include cardinals and robins. Reelfoot Lake boasts the largest population of bald eagles in the country.

Copperhead, rattlesnake, and cottonmouth snakes are a few of the snakes that live in the state. The rivers and lakes have lots of fish, such as trout, largemouth bass, and catfish.

Black bears, white-tailed deer, foxes, rabbits, and squirrels live in Tennessee, too. Wild pigs root around the mountains there.

# Economy

Native Americans in Tennessee lived by fishing and hunting. Later, they planted crops and traded furs. Most of the settlers who moved to the state wanted to farm the land.

Today, not as many people farm, but new machines help those who do to grow more crops. The main crops are tobacco, hay, cotton, and corn. Some farmers raise beef cattle. Many raise horses, too.

## Mining

People have mined for coal in Tennessee for a long time. The coal found there is of very good quality. It can be turned into gas that is used for many purposes.

Tourists to Graceland, Elvis Presley's home, help provide jobs to people in Memphis.

## Big Business

The rivers and streams that run through Tennessee produce electricity. This attracts many businesses to the state. These businesses creates jobs for workers. Factories make clothing, automobiles, and other goods. The state also has many high-tech companies.

## Other Jobs

Some people in the state have service jobs. Some work as doctors, teachers, or bankers. Others work in restaurants, hospitals, or hotels.

## Tourism

Tourism is a growing business in Tennessee. The state has great natural resources and beauty to visit. It also has many historical sites. People also come to hear great music.

## How Money Is Made in Tennessee

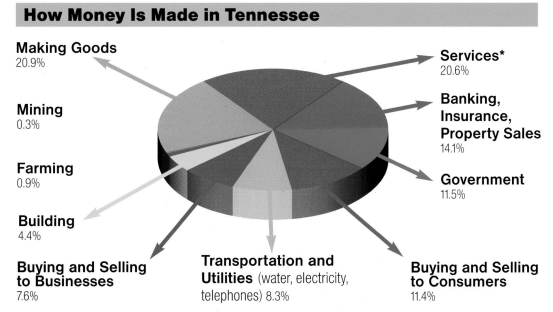

Making Goods
20.9%

Mining
0.3%

Farming
0.9%

Building
4.4%

Buying and Selling to Businesses
7.6%

Transportation and Utilities (water, electricity, telephones) 8.3%

Buying and Selling to Consumers
11.4%

Services*
20.6%

Banking, Insurance, Property Sales
14.1%

Government
11.5%

* Services include jobs in hotels, restaurants, auto repair, medicine, teaching, and entertainment.

## CHAPTER

### 6

# Government

Nashville is Tennessee's capital city. The state's lawmakers work there. The government has three parts, or branches. They are the executive, legislative, and judicial branches.

### Executive Branch

The governor is head of the executive branch. This branch makes sure state laws are carried out. Other people, called **commissioners**, also belong to the executive branch.

### Legislative Branch

The legislative branch makes state laws. The legislature, called the General

The Tennessee State Capitol is in Nashville. It took fourteen years to build. It was completed in 1859.

Assembly, has two parts. They are the senate and the House of Representatives. The two work together.

## Judicial Branch

Judges and courts make up the judicial branch. Judges and courts may decide whether people who have been accused of committing crimes are guilty.

## Local Government

Tennessee has ninety-five counties. Officials elected by the people of the county run each local government.

James K. Polk was the eleventh president of the United States. He served from 1845 to 1849. He was a strong president who kept his promises to the people. President Polk and his wife are buried on the grounds of the State Capitol.

### IN TENNESSEE'S HISTORY

**Tennessee Statesmen**

Three U.S. presidents have come from the state of Tennessee. Andrew Jackson, James K. Polk, and Andrew Johnson all were born in other states, but they worked and lived most of their lives in Tennessee.

# TENNESSEE'S STATE GOVERNMENT

| Executive | | Legislative | | Judicial | |
|---|---|---|---|---|---|
| **Office** | **Length of Term** | **Body** | **Length of Term** | **Court** | **Length of Term** |
| Governor | 4 years | Senate (33 members) | 4 years | Supreme (5 justices) | 8 years |
| | | House of Representatives (99 members) | 2 years | Appeals (12 judges) | 8 years |

# CHAPTER 7

# Things to See and Do

## FUN FACTS

### Lucky Ducks

The Peabody Hotel in Memphis is home to special guests — ducks. In 1930, a worker at the hotel put some ducks in the lobby fountain. The hotel visitors liked the ducks. They have been there ever since. The ducks have their own room in the hotel. With music playing, they march down to the lobby every morning. They return to their room in the late afternoon.

**M**any people know that Tennessee is famous for country music. But the state also has parks, historic sites, crafts, festivals, and sports. All are a part of Tennessee.

## Music

Music is the heart of Tennessee's culture. Nashville is the home of country music. The Grand Ole Opry House is where famous country musicians play. Nashville also has the Country Music Hall of Fame and Museum.

Tennessee has other types of music, too. Bluegrass began in the

Classic bluegrass string instruments hang in the Country Music Hall of Fame in Nashville.

The Grand Ole Opry began as a radio show in 1925. It hosted country western music. Its first home was at Ryman Auditorium in Nashville. In 1974, the new Grand Ole Opry House opened. This photo shows the House at its seventy-fifth birthday party in 2000.

East Tennessee mountains. Blues and jazz grew on the streets of Memphis. And singer Elvis Presley became known as the King of Rock and Roll.

## Nature's Glory

People in Tennessee love the beautiful mountains and valleys. The state has more than fifty state parks. It also has national parks. The Cumberland Gap National Historic Park is on the northeastern border of the state. The Great Smoky Mountains National Park runs along the eastern border. Most of this park is covered in forest. Visitors can hike, bike, or ride horses along the park's trails.

## Museums and Historic Sites

Tennessee has many fine museums to visit. The large cities have art and historic museums. Some museums have folk art, such as pottery and quilts. Other museums, such as the Adventure Science Center in Nashville, are for children to enjoy learning about science. The National Civil Rights Museum is in Memphis.

Many visitors come to see Civil War battlefields and learn about their history. Two famous battlefields are at Shiloh and Stones River.

## Festivals

The state has a strawberry festival and a corn bread festival every year. There also is a storytelling festival and Elvis Week. Arts and crafts festivals are held in many places. One festival even celebrates mules for their hard work!

This cannon stands on Lookout Mountain in southern Tennessee. It is part of the Chickamauga and Chattanooga National Military Park. Two major Civil War battles were fought on this mountain.

## Famous People of Tennessee

# Wilma Rudolph

**Born:** June 23, 1940, St. Bethlehem, Tennessee

**Died:** November 12, 1994, Nashville, Tennessee

Wilma Rudolph was a famous runner. As a child, she was very ill. She needed a leg brace to help her walk. She worked hard to get better. After a long while, Rudolph was able to walk again. She began to run track in high school. She won all the races. She set world records in college. In 1960, Rudolph became the first American woman to win three gold medals in the Olympic Games.

## Sports

Tennessee has many sports teams. Big-league football, basketball, and hockey games are all played here. The Tennessee Titans football team came to Nashville in 1999. They made it to the Super Bowl in 2000. The Memphis Grizzlies play basketball. The Nashville Predators play hockey.

The state has minor-league baseball teams, too. And Tennessee's college sports teams have many loyal fans, especially those from the University of Tennessee.

**border** — an edge or outer part

**colonies** — groups of people living in a new land but governed by the place they came from

**commissioners** — members of government groups or departments

**dams** — barriers built to slow down water flow

**factories** — buildings where goods and products are made

**glaciers** — large bodies of ice that move across land

**Great Depression** — a time, in the 1930s when many people lost jobs and businesses lost money

**independent** — able to act or make a decision without depending on other people

**mounds** — round hills made of earth or stone

**pioneers** — the first people to settle in an area

**plateau** — a large, flat area that is higher than the land around it

**population** — the number of people who live in a place, such as a city, town, or state

**rural** — something that is in the country

**scout** — a person who searches or explores an area to see what is there

**soil** — earth; dirt

**taxes** — money paid by people to the government

**territory** — an area that belongs to a country

**treaty** — a written agreement

## Books

*Davy Crockett: Frontier Hero.* Primary Sources of Famous People in American History (series). J.T. Moriarty (Rosen Publishing)

*Elvis Presley.* Trailblazers of the Modern World (series). Adele Q. Brown (World Almanac Library)

*Knoxville, Tennessee.* Nikki Giovanni (Scholastic Trade)

*Tennessee.* This Land Is Your Land (series). Ann Heinrichs (Compass Point Books)

*Tennessee.* Welcome to the U.S.A. (series). Child's World

*Tennessee Facts and Symbols.* The States and Their Symbols (series). Kathy Feeney (Bridgestone Books)

*Tennessee History Projects: 30 Cool Activities, Crafts, Experiments & More for Kids to Do to Learn about Your State.* Tennessee Experience (series). Carole Marsh (Gallopade International)

## Web Sites

National Civil Rights Museum
www.civilrightsmuseum.org

Tennessee State Museum
www.tnmuseum.org/children

Tennessee: Volunteer State
www.kidskonnect.com/Tennessee/TennesseeHome.html